I0440249

COMMUNIST INFILTRATION

OF AMERICAN CHURCHES

1887 – 2012

World Council of Churches

National Council of Churches

Christine Meinsen

Nothing in this book is intended to give the reader the impression that there are no churches or no pastors faithful to the Word of God as revealed inside the Holy Bible.

God, Himself, has warned us that we must test the spirits to see whether they are of Him. This book testifies to His warning and our need to be vigilant.

Dedicated first to the Glory of God and His Blazing Light of Truth in the Mighty Name of Jesus Christ.

Next, this book is dedicated to every individual who has ever engaged in the ongoing fight to expose and punish Communist activities inside America and suffered the resulting personal attacks launched by these tragically misguided spoilers.

Those of us who realize we are living witnesses to the ongoing progressive attempt to fundamentally transform America are sincerely grateful for the knowledge you continue to share through your countless documented testimonies as well as the suffering and bullying endured by you, your families and friends.

To that end, this author wishes to specifically thank the family of General Albert C. Wedemeyer of the United States Army and all those others who selflessly served on the House Un-American Activities Committee. *The evidence proves you were right.*

The truth isn't always what we want it to be. Still, it must guide our footsteps as we continue the work to secure freedom once more for the next vulnerable, preyed-upon generation.

It's true what they say: *Freedom isn't free.*

Communist Goals (1963)

Congressional Record--Appendix,

pp. A34-A35 January 10, 1963
Current Communist Goals
EXTENSION OF REMARKS OF HON. A. S. HERLONG, JR.
OF FLORIDA
IN THE HOUSE OF REPRESENTATIVES
Thursday, January 10, 1963

Mr. HERLONG. Mr. Speaker, Mrs. Patricia Nordman of De Land, Fla., is an ardent and articulate opponent of communism, and until recently published the De Land Courier, which she dedicated to the purpose of alerting the public to the dangers of communism in America. At Mrs. Nordman's request, I include in the RECORD, under unanimous consent, the following "Current Communist Goals," which she identifies as an excerpt from *The Naked Communist*, by Cleon Skousen:

CURRENT COMMUNIST GOALS

1. U.S. acceptance of coexistence as the only alternative to atomic war.
2. U.S. willingness to capitulate in preference to engaging in atomic war.
3. Develop the illusion that total disarmament [by] the United States would be a demonstration of moral strength.

4. Permit free trade between all nations regardless of Communist affiliation and regardless of whether or not items could be used for war.

5. Extension of long-term loans to Russia and Soviet satellites.

6. Provide American aid to all nations regardless of Communist domination.

7. Grant recognition of Red China. Admission of Red China to the U.N.

8. Set up East and West Germany as separate states in spite of Khrushchev's promise in 1955 to settle the German question by free elections under supervision of the U.N.

9. Prolong the conferences to ban atomic tests because the United States has agreed to suspend tests as long as negotiations are in progress.

10. Allow all Soviet satellites individual representation in the U.N.

11. Promote the U.N. as the only hope for mankind. If its charter is rewritten, demand that it be set up as a one-world government with its own independent armed forces. (Some Communist leaders believe the world can be taken over as easily by the U.N. as by Moscow. Sometimes these two centers compete with each other as they are now doing in the Congo.)

12. Resist any attempt to outlaw the Communist Party. (See cpusa.org)

13. Do away with all loyalty oaths.

14. Continue giving Russia access to the U.S. Patent Office.

15. Capture one or both of the political parties in the United States. (Achieved by Council on Foreign Relations - CFR)

16. Use technical decisions of the courts to weaken basic American institutions by claiming their activities violate civil rights.

17. Get control of the schools. Use them as transmission belts for socialism and current Communist propaganda. Soften the curriculum. Get control of teachers' associations. Put the party line in textbooks.

18. Gain control of all student newspapers.

19. Use student riots to foment public protests against programs or organizations which are under Communist attack.

20. Infiltrate the press. Get control of book-review assignments, editorial writing, policy-making positions.

21. Gain control of key positions in radio, TV, and motion pictures.

22. Continue discrediting American culture by degrading all forms of artistic expression. An American Communist cell was told to "eliminate all good sculpture from parks and buildings, substitute shapeless, awkward and meaningless forms."

23. Control art critics and directors of art museums. "Our plan is to promote ugliness, repulsive, meaningless art."

24. Eliminate all laws governing obscenity by calling them "censorship" and a violation of free speech and free press.

25. Break down cultural standards of morality by

promoting pornography and obscenity in books, magazines, motion pictures, radio, and TV.

26. Present homosexuality, degeneracy and promiscuity as "normal, natural, healthy."

27. Infiltrate the churches and replace revealed religion with "social" religion. Discredit the Bible and emphasize the need for intellectual maturity which does not need a "religious crutch."

28. Eliminate prayer or any phase of religious expression in the schools on the ground that it violates the principle of "separation of church and state."

29. Discredit the American Constitution by calling it inadequate, old-fashioned, out of step with modern needs, a hindrance to cooperation between nations on a worldwide basis.

30. Discredit the American Founding Fathers. Present them as selfish aristocrats who had no concern for the "common man."

31. Belittle all forms of American culture and discourage the teaching of American history on the ground that it was only a minor part of the "big picture." Give more emphasis to Russian history since the Communists took over.

32. Support any socialist movement to give centralized control over any part of the culture--education, social agencies, welfare programs, mental health clinics, etc.

33. Eliminate all laws or procedures which interfere with the operation of the Communist apparatus.

34. Eliminate the House Committee on Un-American Activities.

35. Discredit and eventually dismantle the FBI.

36. Infiltrate and gain control of more unions.

37. Infiltrate and gain control of big business.

38. Transfer some of the powers of arrest from the police to social agencies.

39. Treat all behavioral problems as psychiatric disorders which no one but psychiatrists can understand [or treat].

40. Dominate the psychiatric profession and use mental health laws as a means of gaining coercive control over those who oppose Communist goals.

41. Discredit the family as an institution. Encourage promiscuity and easy divorce.

42. Emphasize the need to raise children away from the negative influence of parents. Attribute prejudices, mental blocks and retarding of children to suppressive influence of parents.

43. Create the impression that violence and insurrection are legitimate aspects of the American tradition; that students and special-interest groups should rise up and use "united force" to solve economic, political or social problems.

44. Overthrow all colonial governments before native populations are ready for self-government.

45. Internationalize the Panama Canal.

46. Repeal the Connally reservation so the United States cannot prevent the World Court from seizing jurisdiction over domestic problems. Give the World Court jurisdiction over nations and individuals alike. (1)

> The beginning of true liberty is Jesus Christ. And therefore the first and last target of all subversion is biblical faith. Hence it is that the Church has been the first target of subversion; and is the most subverted institution in the United States today.
>
> Dr. R.J. Rushdoony

Church Infiltration

Near the end of the 19th Century, at the close of the Civil War, countless American workers were laboring in poverty while "Robber Barons" such as Andrew Carnegie and John D. Rockefeller were harvesting their wealth from the earth's resources. Many viewed the prominent speculators of this time as exploiters of those who helped them gain their riches through backbreaking work, long hours and wages low enough to hold them in desperation and poverty.(2)

A number of the rich justified their cruelty by espousing the damning tenets of Social Darwinism arguing that if evolution favored the survival of the fittest, why then should the strong help the weak to survive? (3)

The "Social Gospel" was born of this time. The intent was to co-opt the churches of that day into a larger, united, organization that would work to alleviate the hardships of the poor. The reality of this "gospel" was located just beneath the word "social" which promoted social-ism and human-ism before the gospel mandate to save souls.

Josiah Strong coordinated the General Christian Conference in 1887 to pool the churches into the Evangelical Alliance for the United States to fuel the fires of the Social Gospel. His primary purpose was to collectivize the churches so "Christian public opinion could make itself felt by the government." Later, this Alliance in Christian Socialism was absorbed by the Federal Council of Churches and the Socialist movement to infiltrate and control Christian churches began in earnest. (4)

Coming from Europe in the 1880's, typical Christian Socialist organizations were: Church Association for the Advance of Labor, 1887; Society of Christian Socialists, 1889; and the Christian Socialist Fellowship. Each of these groups eventually melded into the Federal Council of Churches. Since that time, for more than one-hundred-twenty years, their primary goal has been to unite all churches under one umbrella thereby forming a world church.

A young man named Walter Rauschenbusch graduated from the prestigious Rochester Theological Seminary in 1885, thoroughly indoctrinated in the Socialist tenets of "Illuminism" – a philosophy purporting to be religious but one which substituted faith in man where faith in God should stand. Karl Marx noted that "Illuminism is really nothing else but Marxism." Rauschenbusch was considered to be both an Illuminist and a Marxist. (5)

In 1892, the Rev. Walter Rauschenbusch, author of *Christianity and the Social Crisis*, organized the "Brotherhood of the Kingdom" with several fellow travelers to promote socialism and humanism in American churches and to reform the institutions of capitalism. Rauschenbusch is considered to be the "real founder of social Christianity." (6)

On **September 11,** 1893, the first World's Parliament of Religions was held in Chicago, Illinois. According to the records, "men of progress" from all over the globe gathered together in what would come to be known as the first outward steps to unite the world's religions. One specific question went unanswered. How could the representative of one religion affirm the beliefs of another without denying his own? If a Christian affirmed Judaism, was he not denying Jesus Christ? If a Muslim affirmed the beliefs of a Jew, was he not turning against his entire culture?

Rauschenbusch, later a professor at Rochester Theological Seminary, taught his socialistic religious philosophy to future clergymen. In 1893 he proclaimed, "The only power that can make socialism succeed... is religion. It cannot work in an irreligious country." He declared, "Socialism is coming," proclaiming that it would come "creatively in the social process without recourse to illegality or violence." (7)

Meanwhile, the Reverend F. D. Huntington, another Marxist, was in New York setting up the Christian Socialist Movement as an offshoot of London's Fabian Socialist Society. Radical eugenicist George Bernard Shaw, Sidney and Beatrice Webb and several other notable Marxists had earlier directed the creation of the demented Fabian group. It has been reported that the Webbs traveled to America in 1898 to review the success of Fabian infiltration of our religious institutions. (8)

In 1901, a collection of Socialists and Fabians took leadership positions in the newly created National Federation of Churches. Dr. Harry F. Ward was among these. In his later years, Ward secured several powerful roles in various church councils and in the Methodist Church. The Inter-Church Conference on Federation proposed a Federal Council of Churches in 1905. The American Institute of Marxist Studies (AIMS) published a book titled, "Marxism and Christianity" by Herbert Apthekers as a tribute to AIMS Honorary Chairman, Dr. Harry F. Ward which contains a full page engraved picture of Ward on its dedication page. (9)

In 1907, Ward set up the Methodist Federation for Social Services as a supporting front for the International Church Conference. Then in 1908, Ward and Rauschenbusch, together, formed the Federal Council of Churches. Believing that "Socialism must start in the churches," the Constitution of the Inter-Church Conference adopted the "Social Creed of the Churches."

Forty-four years later, the House Committee on Un-American Activities cited the Methodist Federation for Social Services for "having been Communist-controlled since its inception" due to its objective "to transform the Methodist Church and Christianity into an instrument for the achievement of Socialism." There were claims by some that the Creed had been approved by Nikolai Lenin and a study of the creed demonstrates its compatibility with Marxism and Communism. (10)

In 1924 and 1929, Harry Ward traveled to Moscow where he met with Stalin to discuss the use of American churches to further the International cause of Communism. In 1925, Ward gave a series of lectures to clergymen in China. These lectures were discussed at length in Russia's Comintern, the central operating power for Communism, where agreement was reached that "the missions and church institutions in China could be used… to cover up Communist espionage activities…" By now, the Federal Church Council had an office in Washington with a budget of $350,000.00. (11)

The Naval Institute Proceedings in 1928 confirmed that the Federal Council consistently meddled in matters of defense and was "probably the most powerful propaganda organization in the country." (12)

Congressman George Tinkham revealed in his testimony before the Senate Lobbying Investigating Committee that he had received such propaganda no fewer than 15 times. Tinkham revealed at a later date that John D. Rockefeller Jr. had contributed over $137,000 to the Federal Council between 1926 and 1929 – which was equal to approximately ten percent of the Council's total reported annual income. (13)

From 1908 to 1932, the Federal Council grew and prospered while still maintaining ties with Marxists and Fabian Socialists. The Council often created or endorsed similar groups such as the Church Peace Union and the Fellowship for Reconciliation. Investigations by Congressional and Military Intelligence revealed the subversive nature of the Council. A resolution was introduced to Congress in 1927 by Congressman Arthur Free calling the Federal Council "a communist organization aimed at establishing a state-church."

U. S. Army Intelligence further exposed the Council's activities in 1932 in testimony given before the House of Representatives Immigration Committee that linked Council officials with "the most extreme Communists." In fact, the August 13, 1932 issue of the "Sunday School

Times" exposed an obscene sex manual distributed by the Council calling it "a crowning achievement... for atheist Communism." Congressional Committee Report No. 2290 formally listed the Council as a subversive organization. (14)

The Office of Naval Intelligence reported that the Council gave "aid and comfort to the Communist movement" in 1935 and said the Council was extremely "active against national defense." This same year, after finishing eighteen month training courses in Moscow, two union leaders, Victor and Walter Reuther, became the Council's experts on labor relations. The Reuthers sent a letter to friends in America instructing them to "carry on the fight for a Soviet America." It was later reported that Walter Reuther declared in a speech in Flint, Michigan, "We do not believe in God, but man is god." (15)

It was in 1942 at the very beginning of World War II, prior to the formation of the United Nations under Communist leaders like Alger Hiss, when the council revealed the coming agenda for a centrally controlled world government through the issuance of a public proclamation on internationalism, military matters, and economic affairs specifically calling for: a world government; strong limits on national sovereignty; international control of all armed forces; a universal monetary system; and a single international bank. Additionally, the Council sought a world policed by an international army and navy. This same year, the

Council held a "Peace Study Conference" stating, "Many duties performed by state and national governments can now be effectively carried out only by international authority." (16)

Reflecting back to the time of World War II, the United States was allied with Communist Russia against Nazi Germany.

In 1945, the Federal Council of Churches sent delegates to San Francisco to aid in the founding of the United Nations where Communist Agent, Alger Hiss, played an important role. Hiss had earlier served as a chairman of an influential committee of the Federal Council. (17) Article 15, Section 3 of the UN Charter states specifically that freedom of religion may be subject to such *limitations as are prescribed by law.*

In the 1950's and 1960's, NCC funneled money through its relief agency, the Church World Service to help fund Communist regimes in Yugoslavia and Poland. (18)

Select delegates from 147 churches, mostly from Europe and North America, met in Amsterdam in 1948 to form the World Council of Churches (WCC). (19) The World Council of Churches is now the parent organization of the National Council of Churches operating inside the United States of America.

It is important to understand that Communists agitate society for change by creating divisions among her people and highlighting her ills. If a person of color (not white) becomes the victim of a violent crime or a person of a certain religious affiliation (not Christian) becomes the victim of a violent crime, it will be designated a hate crime and repeated on every news station morning, noon and night and reported in every major newspaper across the country. Within three hours of the breaking news, Communists will have alerted their sister organizations and set up a bank account to receive donations in the name of the victim. Worse even still, they will prey upon the vulnerable family members of the victim, offer their support and co-opt them into their ranks by catapulting them to near fame on the speaker circuit. Communists spare no one from their deceitful cause.

Since at least the mid 19th century, Communists have worked to divide and conquer America by separating her people into groups while constantly delivering the message that any uncomfortable or negative occurrence in their lives is the result of unseen and unverified prejudice at the hands of Capitalists, whites and/or Christians because these groups represent to them their most formidable enemy. In fact, it is the Christian Bible that taught man freedom and if the world had never been blessed with the teachings of Jesus Christ, there would be no nation on earth that could lay claim to a decisive reason for respecting human life.

Communists, often trained from childhood, believe they are at war with these later mentioned "groups." They are called to work unceasingly for "the cause" of some utopia they believe man can achieve without divine intervention in a world full of sin. Here we find the man that is often given over to his delusions and thereby rendered unable to discern the consequences of the ultimate gamble upon which he tosses the dice of his eternity never realizing that if there is no God, he will never know it because upon his singular meaningless death his brain will stop and he will cease to think. He will never know that he was correct yet if he has chosen unwisely...

The Christian, if wrong, would also never know it. He faces no threat yet, if correct, he inherits the Kingdom of a Loving God.

In the book, *Introducing the World Council of Churches*, by Marlin VanElderen, published by WCC Publications in Geneva, it explains "...the heart of what the WCC is all about is its engagement on behalf of the 'sinned-against' in the struggle for justice. This engagement may take the form of empowering... organizations of people who are oppressed because of their race.... may involve expert analysis and prophetic exposure of social and economic and political powers that control the lives of millions of people... it may be expressed by encouraging and enabling a small and marginalized community... to take charge of its own future... The life of the World Council of Churches is nurtured by the vision *'that all may be one'*... Some would accent the importance of the Council's global constituency: WCC member churches are found in every part of the world. Especially in Asia and the Middle East... Moreover, the agenda of the World Council is a changing one... Ten or twenty years ago there was little if any concern in most churches about many issues that seem very important today: AIDS, new religious movements, the international debt crisis (the "debt crisis" never disappears), inclusive language, the 'greenhouse effect', to mention only a few."

Van Elderen, having not the prophetic eyes to see and ears to hear, failed to report the deadly mayhem spread over the earth by Communists throughout their history.

The WCC is a proponent of Liberation Theology, was infiltrated by the KGB during the Cold War, has funded Marxist insurgents throughout the world and continually calls for capitalism to be "reformed" according to socialist principles. (20)

Severe criticism was levied against the Federal Council of Churches by concerned Americans so, the leaders decided, as per the pattern of Communist policy and practice, to simply change the name of the organization. In 1950, the Council dissolved and the National Council of Churches was born absorbing four more agencies including the radical Church World Service. Leaders were maintained and transferred to the new group admitting that "all work of the Federal Council will continue under new auspices." (21)

The Committee on Un-American Activities found that eleven of the twenty-nine clergymen who served as leaders and had signed their churches into the NCC had records of affiliations with pro-communist causes. A clear thirty-four percent were tied to communist projects. At a bare minimum, 700 officers, representatives and staff members had communist front records. (22)

In 1952, the National Council published the Revised Standard Version of the Bible. Dr. Luther A. Weigle, a man with a record of six affiliations with leftist organizations, who had previously assisted Unitarians in crafting Sunday School texts, served as chairman of the committee credited with this work. Seven other members of the committee also had records of leftist and pro-communist affiliations. (23)

Testifying before the House Committee on Un-American Activities in 1953, Communist Benjamin Gitlow admitted that members of the clergy "wielded tremendous influence in the religious field and did Trojan Horse work in advancing the Communist conspiracy in religion." Gitlow also said the most important Communist in the field of religion was Robert W. Dunn who "served as the Communist Party's liaison between its political committee and secretariat and the clergymen operating under instructions of the Party." Dunn was an official of the American Civil Liberties Union (ACLU). Additionally, Communist leader Joseph Kornfeder, who had trained at the Lenin School of

Political Warfare in Moscow from 1927 to 1930 and served as a top aide to Josef Stalin, testified that there were nearly 600 American clergymen who were members of the Communist Party. (24)

After Dwight Eisenhower was sworn in as America's president, radical leftists from the National Council of Churches were placed in key posts. For instance, John Foster Dulles became the Secretary of State; Arthur Flemming became head of the manpower division of the Department of Defense then later Secretary of Health, Education and Welfare; Harold Stassen once the Vice President of NCC and President of its International Council of Religious Education became Mutual Security Director. (25)

None of this should be surprising because it is a pattern of behavior: its policy and practice of the American government. Consider that *after* Soviet agent Harry Dexter White, Under-Secretary of the U. S. Treasury during World War II, was discovered he was re-assigned to serve as the new Executive Director of the U. S. Mission to the International Monetary Fund of the United Nations. He also received a pay raise! The story goes that J. Edgar Hoover, Director of the FBI who spent years of his life studying and hunting down Communists (before they customarily destroyed his reputation) was amazed but "Attorney General Herbert Brownell, Jr. stated publicly that President Truman knew White was a Soviet spy when he made the appointment." Soon after, the chairman of the Federal Reserve Board began pushing for economic aid and comfort to Communist China. (26)

Expanding its activities in 1958, the NCC put forth its "World Order Study Conference" advocating: universal disarmament; permanent UN police forces; ratification of the Genocide convention; internationalism to supersede national patriotism; avoid hostility toward communist countries; abolishment of universal military training and the draft; expanded trade with communist countries, the welcoming of Red China into the UN; the suspension of nuclear testing; abandonment of overseas military bases; and abolishment of the House Committee on Un-American Activities that was rounding them up and prosecuting them for their treasonous activities. (27)

Dr. Cynthia Wedel, Associate Director of the Center for a Voluntary Society, a pioneer organization in the study of sensitivity training, became president of the NCC in 1969. Wedel was also a leading member of the subversive Jeanette Rankin Brigade named for its members who were wives and daughters of communists. Wedel's husband, the Rev. Canon Theodore O. Wedel, signed a communist petition in 1957 and had been discovered supporting communist causes since 1940. (28)

Exposed in 1960 in the United States House of Representatives was a pamphlet bibliography of 260 children's books, authored by known communists, which had been published by the National Council's Department of Racial and Cultural Relations in 1957. Alfred S. Kramer stated in the foreword, "We of the National Council... consider... these books... safe to recommend to children." Authors included Communists W.E.B. DuBois, Shirley Graham, Herbert Aptheker, Langston Hughes and Victor Perlo. One book by Langston Hugues contained an outrageous poem named, "Goodbye Christ." (29)

1964 was the year the NCC's Commission on Religion and Race sponsored a youth ministry consultation at the Methodist General Board of Education in Nashville, Tennessee to enlist young people in violent political agitations telling them they must be bloodied in disorders for the cause of racial equality; that they were slaves to their parents; that they must be freed from this bondage and that if stopped by police, they should be proud. Here, we should remember a few of Stalin's instructions: "Give the teenage drugs, alcohol, praise his wildness; strangle him with sex; give him complete freedom everywhere. *If we kill the national pride and patriotism of just one generation, we will have won the country.*" (30)

Remaining vigilant to the cause of Communism, NCC representatives testified before Congressional Committees *against voluntary* prayer and Bible reading in America's schools in 1966. (31)

School shootings later followed. As if this outcome

could be expected from a society that ignored God's guidance, government agents responded by moving such tragedies to the "expected" category. This was well demonstrated by the allocation of taxpayer dollars designated to fund additional on site counseling teams readied to converge on schoolchildren when such violence recurred. These often haphazardly trained individuals gathered data regarding students' thoughts, feelings and actions after such violent and often deadly events. A door was shoved open and the big, hairy toe of Adolph Hitler's "Death Education" came to America through books like *Death and Dying Education* by Richard O. Ulin, A National Education Association (teachers' union) publication. Not only were students forced to cope with the loss of brothers, sisters, friends, classmates and teachers but, they were forced by government agents to discuss *their own suicides* and coerced to craft *their own obituaries* while their parents labored away to fund the government that funded the schools that funded the teachers and counselors, that funded the curriculum that hurt the children that lived in the house that rebellion built.

September 15, 1967, NCC issued a resolution opposing Americans' right to keep and bear arms calling for tighter controls on all firearms at the state and federal levels. (32)

NCC issued the Policy Statement: "Imperatives of Peace and Responsibility of Power" on February 21, 1968 advocating that the power of the United States should be used to advance the global government of the United Nations. This statement also condemned America for improperly hoarding its sovereignty and for reservations about using the newly established World Court. (33)

"Christian Challenges" magazine, April 1971, published an article by Dorothy Faber of the Foundation for Christian Theology informing the public that the Council had begun active propaganda in support of Communist Cuba by issuing packets on Cuba from the World Church Center in New York. This NCC packet contained a list of recommended reading which was pro-Castro and contained a booklet by mass-murderer Che Guevara. Just two packet items were religious and each was an excerpt from a Castro publication. (34)

In mid 1971, G. Russell Evans, author of *Apathy, Apostasy and Apostles,* studied the activities herein described and sent individual letters to seven high officials of the NCC's General Board in the New York headquarters seeking answers to questions about their activities. In his letter he asked, "Do you think the preservation of America is important to the continuance of Christianity? Do you believe that the communists intend to dominate the world? Do you believe the 'able-bodied' should get welfare handouts?" Evans reported that, "three of the seven officials acknowledged the letter, stating in effect that they did not have time to answer the questions and that more information should be obtained from the New York office." He never received any response from the other four.

NCC's General Assembly meeting was held in Dallas in 1972. NCC members elected Rev. W. Sterling Cary of New York, a district ministerial executive for the United Church of Christ, to serve as their new president. Cary was a signer to James Forman's "Black Manifesto" in 1969 which was a written demand for churches and synagogues to pay blacks reparations for prior wrongs. After being elected as president of NCC, Cary disgraced America and the principles of truth by ranting that "Conditions are worse now" as if he were totally unaware of the advances that led blacks out of slavery and into Congress and every level of society. (35)

An entire directory of black officeholders who served during the Reconstruction era in the 1800's, *Freedom's Lawmakers* by Eric Foner, 1996, explains that *1,510 black men served in all levels of local, state and federal government before being deleted from our history books* and denied their earned right to be celebrated as original founders of America. Foner believes there are hundreds more who have yet to have their records discovered and published. In his acknowledgements, Foner thanks "the U.S. Census published in Utah by Accelerated Indexing Systems and Precision Indexing Company, and the generosity of the Mormon Church's Genealogical Library in Los Angeles (for) providing access to their extensive collections" which he writes made it "possible to locate over a thousand black officeholders in the manuscript census for 1870." Among others, Foner also cites the *Black Biographical Dictionaries, 1790 – 1950*, edited by Randall K. Burkett, Nancy Hall Burkett and Henry Louis Gates, Jr. as "an indispensible source for anyone tracking down information about black Americans. Foner found that *by 1877 "around 2,000 black men had held federal, state, and local public offices, ranging from member of Congress to justice of the peace."* (36)

Oh, yes, America's black population has been unfairly slighted - just not by the people accused by the leading Communist agitators. One must go back to study the people who founded some of our most well-known segregated black groups like the NAACP to understand the true purpose of these groups that spread the lies that deceive the masses about the proud heritage of America's black patriots.

Suppressing the truth has always been a key component of the Communist movement that seeks to divide and conquer America. As with every labeled group, Communists believe they need to anger black Americans so they in turn can be used to agitate society for change without ever understanding the change they will receive or who is designing that change. In reality, what most blacks seek is a return to the past! Racism was nearly conquered in America in the 1800's only to be revived by the Communist infiltrators inside the Democratic Party! One of the best books on these facts is *Setting the Record Straight: American History in Black*

& *White,* by David Barton, 2004 which is available at wallbuilders.com. This book is full of fascinating, censored truths about the tragic, deceitful history of the Democratic Party that continues its militant rampage of deception to further its self centered goals to this day.

Suffice to say that every American has heard the lies about black history perpetrated by Communist agitators and those lies have altered the course of America in an extremely criminal way causing magnificent injury to every black child who should have known their ancestors loved the freedom they ultimately found in America – they fought for it alongside Indian & Caucasian soldiers! These people of different skin colors *trusted each other with their lives in the shared struggle for liberty and, together, they were victorious!*

Nevertheless, NCC President, W. Sterling Cary of New York, served as chairman of the pre-planning for the 1972 Assembly meeting where black racist Leroi Jones was a featured speaker. Leroi who later began using the name Imamu Amira Baraka, was a pornographic poet, a militant activist and an anti-Semitic writer. Jones' belted out a 90 minute racist diatribe full of anti-American, anti-white sentiments. Meanwhile, back home in Newark, N.J., Jones' non-Christian Temple Kawaida was receiving federal taxpayer money to the tune of 6.4 million dollars for an apartment project! (37)

Methodist Bishop James Armstrong led a delegation of American church officials to Cuba and was later elected

President of the NCC. In 1977, after his trip to Cuba Armstrong announced, "There is a significant difference between situations where people are imprisoned for opposing regimes designed to perpetuate inequities, and in Chile and Brazil, for example, and situations where people are imprisoned for opposing regimes designed to remove inequities, as in Cuba." (38) Neither Armstrong nor his accomplices mentioned that Castro rationed the rice of the Cuban people; held them in poverty and forbade them to utter a single word against his murderous regime.

Documents seized from El Salvador guerrilla fighters in 1983 proved that between 1981 and 1983, NCC through its Evangelical Committee for Aid to Development, an organization established to dole out donations from collection plates in American churches and whose leadership opening professed solidarity with the Sandinistas' Marxist aims, contributed nearly $400,000 to the Sandinista Party. (39)

By now a new catalyst for global government had been well established by Albert Gore Jr. who jetted around the world spreading his enormous "carbon footprint" along with his dire message that the sky was falling and the earth was sinking. Al had invested in several companies that were positioned to make him a trillionaire if only the world would leap into his snare. Among these companies were Emerald Cities Investment and Chicago Climate Exchange which, during his tenure with the Joyce Foundation, Barak

Hussein Obama had also directed wads of cash per numerous reports including one titled "Crime, Inc." by Glenn Beck. Mankind need only to recognize that the omni-benevolent United Nations, founded by known Communists like Alger Hiss, could save us all from impending disaster through world-wide legislation known as Sustainable Development and Agenda 21.

For all its controlling, unwanted legislation… *Green was fast becoming the new red.*

Of course, NCC jumped on board. In 1998, Joan Brown Campbell, then General Secretary of NCC, touted the virtues of the radical environmental movement's allegations about man-caused global warming ranting that belief in the money-making hoax should be a "litmus test for the faith community." (40)

When anti-second Amendment activists gathered in Washington, D. C. for the Million Mom March in May of 2000, they carried the endorsement of NCC. Leaders of the protest evolved into a national organization under the same name which is now a member group of America Votes which promotes environmental extremism, open borders and radical left-wing agendas of teachers' unions. (41)

The Christian group "One Million Moms" is *not* affiliated with the Million Mom organization that organized the march.

Religious leaders from all over the world gathered for

the Millennium World Peace Summit of Religious and Spiritual Leaders at the United Nations Building in New York City from August 28 - 31, 2000 where they signed a pledge with 8 promises. The event was the brainchild of billionaire, CNN founder Ted Turner who served as the honorary chair. Turner blasphemed the entire meaning of the life, death and resurrection of Jesus Christ when he told the crowd: "The thing that disturbed me was that my religion, the Christian sect, was very intolerant, not of religious freedom, but we thought we were the only ones going to heaven." (42)

If Turner had ever been a Christian, his speech proved he missed the message in its entirety. Nothing could be considered more tolerant than to lay down your life so that others might live - even those who mock you, torture you and murder you. Christ's gift of eternal life is available to *all*.

Religion is man's attempt to reach God. Christianity is God's attempt to reach man.

In Ted Turner's home state, Georgia, the *"New Ten Commandments"* are displayed on nineteen foot high carved stones as a mockery to God's Ten Commandments as per the tablets given to Moses, America's first founding father. These new occult commandments were ordered in June, 1979 by a well-dressed, articulate stranger who commissioned Elberton Granite Finishing Company in Elbert County Georgia to build the edifice to transmit a message to mankind in eight different languages. While stating that his name was R. C. Christian, this man declared that he represented a group of men who wanted to offer direction to humanity. The stone-maker later refused to reveal the true identity of the customer responsible for the pagan declarations which cover the topics of governance through the establishment of a world government; population and reproduction control; the environment and man's relationship to nature and spirituality. Here is the dream for mankind carved in the Georgia Guide Stones known as the:

New 10 Commandments

1. *Maintain* humanity *under* 500,000,000 in perpetual balance with nature.
2. *Guide* reproduction wisely – improving fitness and diversity.
3. Unite humanity with a *living new* language.
4. *Rule* passion – *faith* – tradition – and all things with tempered reason.
5. Protect people and nations with fair *laws* and just *courts.*
6. Let all nations *rule* internally resolving external disputes in a *world court*.
7. Avoid petty laws and *useless* officials.
8. Balance personal *rights* with social *duties*.
9. Prize truth – beauty – love – seeking *harmony with the infinite.*
10. Be not a *cancer* on the earth – Leave room for nature – Leave room for nature.

The "keystone" states "Let these be guidestones to an age of reason." (43)

Humanism offers quite an improvement from God's 10 Commandments – right? No more thou shalt not kill, thou shalt not steal, thou shalt not covet thy neighbor's wife, no honor thy father and thy mother. Not in the new *season of reason.*

If man is killing *Mother* Earth, what must be done with man? Might we have just seen the elite's answer in "commandment" number one?

During the Christmas season in 2011, Mercedes Benz repeatedly aired an ad on television that proved their sales execs had joined elites in opposite world. The ad proclaimed, "The Season of Reason."

After the September 11, 2001 terrorist attacks, NCC became a signatory to a document dated November 1, 2001 that characterized the terrorist attack as a legal matter suggesting it should be addressed through criminal-justice procedures rather than military reprisals. Blaming social injustices for the protesting actions of the homicidal hijackers this document declared, "security and justice are mutually reinforcing goals that ultimately depend upon the promotion of all human rights for all people" calling on America "to promote fundamental rights around the world." (44)

Surely excited to push green as the new red, in 2002, NCC promoted the morally reprehensible "What Would

Jesus Drive?" campaign. (45) Thank goodness, the company knew better than to ask what Muhammad would drive.

NCC General Secretary Robert Edgar sent a request to the U.S. Department of Defense on December 8, 2003 requesting permission to send an interfaith delegation to visit terrorists being held in Guantanamo Bay. Declaring that the Council would "continue to advocate for the due process rights of Guantanamo Bay detainees," NCC joined in "a broad coalition of domestic and international religious, legal and human rights organizations filing a friend of the court brief in a Supreme Court case wherein they asserted that foreign nationals being held at Guantanamo Bay have the right to challenge their detention." (46)

Leaving no ruthless, totalitarian stone unturned, it was in February, 2005 when the Communist NCC joined Muslim Imams, clerics and radicals in condemning Israel for having "established hundreds upon hundreds of checkpoints, roadblocks, and gates across the Occupied Territories, making daily life and travel extremely difficult for ordinary Palestinians." (47) Leaders of the NCC failed to mention that fully 70% of Arabs in the West Bank and Gaza approve of murder via suicide bombings, that there is no trace of an Arab peace movement urging a halt to terror attacks, that Palestinians in Israel enjoy more civil, political and human rights than in any other Arab nation on earth; that Israel came to own the West Bank and Gaza not because of political impulse but because of its victory in the 1967 war when attacked by Egypt, Jordan and Syria and the subsequent war brought against Israel when a coalition of Arab armies attacked in 1973, nor that when Egypt, the spearhead in that war became the only nation to agree to peace talks; *Israel returned Sinai with all its oil.* (48)

NCC's Robert Edgar rallied with other Christians and Jewish leaders in Washington, D.C. in March, 2006 in a show of support for legislation that would legalize illegal aliens inside the United States no matter their country of origin or their intentions during a declared Holy Jihad against all non-Muslim human beings regardless of race, age, sex and socio-economic status. (49)

In Rosemont, Illinois, August, 2007, NCC's Interfaith Relations Office sponsored an Ecumenical Study Seminar at the 44th Annual Convention of the Islamic Society for North America (ISNA) for "reflecting and learning together." (50)

Mark D. Tooley, President of the Institute on Religion and Democracy and author of *Taking Back the United Methodist Church*, posted an article on February 21, 2008 entitled, "The Church of Global Warming" explaining that the NCC had taken "its Global Warming alarmism to Northern Ireland." He reported the NCC's eager "mission was sponsored by the British Consulate in New York" and other participants of the 2 day junket "were the Catholic Coalition on Climate Change, the

Coalition on the Environment and Jewish Life and the Presbyterian Church (USA)." Today, many of Northern Ireland's churches are becoming eco-congregations. (51)

Cassandra Carmichael, director of NCC's eco-justice program alleged, "Because global climate change will effect (sic) us all, and those in poverty the most, it transcends religious and political divides" providing vibrant opportunities for faith communities to come together to address this global concern." (52)

In 2007, during the World Church Council's "Decade to Oppose Violence," the WCC sent four solidarity delegates called "Living Letters" to the United States to investigate America's "violence" which includes the lack of total gun control, U. S. international arms sales and the war in Iraq. This team included a Pakistani human rights lawyer, a Lebanese hospital executive, a South African ecumenical leader and a Brazilian ecumenist who visited Washington D. C., New York, Philadelphia and New Orleans. (53)

While in D. C., NCC President Michael Livingston told the team, "We need your help to turn around this terrible situation we have... We want to learn from you... to make this world a world of peace." Also present was Ladd Everitt of the Coalition to Stop Gun Violence who argued, "We have a real pride in violence in our country... We... profit from it." (54)

Of course, there was no mention of the fact that the

"peace movement" is really the "transfer power movement" in that no weapons are actually disarmed – only nations. Weapons, including nuclear bombs, are transferred to the all-powerful United Nations leaving all individual nation states unable to defend themselves against this radically tyrannical One World Government that is falsely portrayed as sloppy and inept by the morally bankrupt fifth pillar: the media. In truth, the U. N. rules through unelected boards and some 80,000 non-governmental organizations with "consultative status." By definition, these unelected committees, boards, panels and organizations are "Soviet Satellites" or "Soviets" that construct laws while remaining unseen and unaccountable to the people.

The 4 "Letters" visited our nation's capital where they were overwhelmed at the violence depicted in our memorials. The Brazilian exclaimed that the "contrast between the founding values of this nation and the policies of today were evident." It was reported that questions were raised about our celebration of violence including these insinuating gems: "Victory and sacrifice are the only ways to build a great nation?" And, why is it that the "cost of freedom is paid by so many human lives." (55) It's as if these infamous four were so stupid they were devoid of the knowledge that more than *two-hundred-million lives became the victims of genocides committed by madmen who espoused the utopia of Communism* in their insatiable desires to rule over others: as if China, Iran, Iraq, Egypt, North Korea, North

Vietnam, Cuba, Venezuela and every other murderous regime did not exist. Reality is simply an inconvenient truth to be brushed aside for their ignorant, deceitful, selfish political agendas.

Today, NCC claims that its members include 35 Protestant, Anglican and Orthodox Christian denominations, and approximately 50 million members from over 140 congregations. Among these are the Presbyterian Church USA, the United Church of Christ, the Episcopal Church, the United Methodist Church, the Evangelical Lutheran Church in America and the American Baptists Churches in the USA. (56)

A large portion of funding for the National Council of Churches comes from the collection plates in member churches yet most congregants have no idea that they are supporting causes that undermine their families, their nation, their world and the souls of the masses. Other funding comes from some of the most radical leftist groups and foundations in America including the usual suspects: the United Nations Foundation, the Sierra Club, TrueMajority, ACORN, People for the American Way, MoveOn.org and the Connect US Network with ties to George Soros' Open Society Institute, the Tides Foundation, the Rockefeller Brothers Fund, the Carnegie Corporation of New York, the Ford Foundation, the Rasmussen Foundation, the W. K. Kellogg Foundation, the Annie E. Casey Foundation, the Beldon Fund and the Lilly Endowment. (57)

The Institute on Religion and Democracy (IRD) states that the NCC "is more dependent financially upon the Ford Foundation than upon 32 of its 35 member denominations" and that "Most of the NCC-supporting groups share several characteristics: a) they are not affiliated with an NCC member communion, or any other church. In 1999 NCC asked the United Methodist Church to increase its yearly contribution of $2.5 million to $3.2 million. (58)

In September 2002, the United Nations hosted the Global Peace Summit for Women in Geneva, Switzerland which welcomed hundreds of female religious leaders from various nations and religious persuasions. Although some professed to be Christians, reports of the event told a different story. Robert Maginnis, former director of the Family Research Council reported, "… the hidden agenda was to unite people under one religious umbrella so they would more peacefully accept the UN's radical political goals… I can see the possibility that it's the globalization of world religion." CBN News reporter Wendy Griffith filed a report titled "Ushering in the One-World Religion," wherein she stated that "it was clear that Jesus was not invited… Christian scholars say the Bible warns of a time when the entire world will unite under a false global religious and political system… it appears the UN could be taking the first steps in that direction." (59) As we have learned here, she was right and wrong: right in that they seek to unite all religions into a global political system, wrong in that this could be the UN's "first steps" toward that goal.

Alleged Christian minister Joan Brown Campbell co-chair of the Global Peace Initiative lit a candle then spoke about peace and "harnessing their feminine energies" to bring peace to a damaged planet yet never mentioned Jesus Christ. When questioned about this huge omission, Campbell responded, "That's not a purposeful intent. This is a meeting, of course, of people of all religions... I mean everyone here would say there is a God; this is not a group of Atheists, this is a group of people of faith, and for everyone there is a god-person by whatever name." (60)

A "god-person?" That's an oxymoron.

Maginnis summarized the United Nations' religious summit – that failed to recognize Christ – saying: "**The name of Jesus has power** and that's why *Satan doesn't like it; he doesn't want to hear it in the halls of the UN,* whether it be in New York City or in Geneva. So when Ms. Campbell presents herself as a representative for Christians, where does the name Christian come from? It comes from Jesus Christ, the Lord and Savior; and if you don't invoke His name in the context of religion, then I think you've fallen far short and clearly you've done a disservice to Christianity because He is the center of our salvation." (61)

The Greenhouse Crisis Foundation and the Eco-Justice

Working Group of the National Council of Churches published *101 Ways to Help Save the Earth*, a guide which provides "Fifty-two Weeks of Congregational Activities to Save the Earth" and purges the world of all remnants of the Christian calendar. Christmas and Easter are replaced with new holidays such as "Earth Day" and "World Environment Day." Mother's Day transforms to "Gaia Day" and citizens under the new global government are asked to "Include images of the Earth as 'mother' in (their) celebrations." Our 4th of July is remade into a day to celebrate "Freedom from Pollution." Thanksgiving remains but we are to "Give thanks for the gift of food from the environment and for those who produce it." (62)

April 22 is "Earth Day." It is also Vladimir Lenin's birthday.

The Joint Appeal by Religion and Science for the Environment issued their "Declaration of the 'Mission to Washington'" May 12, 1992 with leaders of faith groups, government, prestigious universities and environmental groups including the Wilderness Society, the Union of Concerned Scientists, Wangari Maathai and her Green Belt Movement, the Natural Resources Defense Council, the Rainforest Alliance and the World Resources Institute. Paul Gorman, the progressive environmentalist and pop scientist Carl Saga co-chaired the event. The "Declaration" condemned America as "the leading polluter on Earth" which "generat(es) more greenhouse gasses, especially CO2, than any other country." The signatories advocated that America bore the most responsibility to affect global environmental change which means that she should sacrifice most and provide the most funding. (63) (Strange since America is now 15 trillion dollars in debt and must borrow money from Communist China where there is so much pollution the government forbid the Chinese people from driving cars before and during the Olympics because the thick grey air would be viewed by millions across the globe via their television screens.) Subsequently, a number of resolutions were issued, one in particular forming the National Religious Partnership for the Environment (NRPE) whose formal founders are global warming beneficiaries Al Gore, Paul Gorman, Carl Sagan, Dean James Morton and Joan Brown Campbell from the NCC. (64)

Individuals who heavily influenced the founding of the NRPE included: Bishop James W. Malone, who helped to found Kim Bobo's Interfaith Worker Justice network in 1996; John Carr, longtime board member of the Center for Community Change and activist of the Catholic Conference that worked in partnership with John Sweeney of the AFL-CIO and Ernesto Cortes of the Saul Alinsky founded Industrial Areas Foundation and Dr. Ronald Sider, director of Evangelicals for Social Action. (65)

Per DiscoverTheNetworks.org, "As of mid-2010, five of NRPE's six trustees were still signatories of the original Declaration. These included Rev. Dr. John Brown

Campbell; John Carr; Ronald Sider; Dr. John Ruskay, Executive Vice President & CEO of the UJA Federation of New York since 1999; and Rabbi David Saperstein, Director of the Religious Action Center of Reform Judaism, co-founder of the Faith in Public Life network, and board member for the NAACP and the People for the American Way. Rounding out the board was Rev. Dr. Michael Kinnamon, the General Secretary of the National Council of Churches U.S.A." (66)

NRPE warns that we "are wounding God's creation" and in order to prevent cataclysmic horror we must undergo a fundamental transformation of "our cities and transportation systems in the direction of a sustainable economy." Further Gorman advises that green legislation alone will not solve the crisis: "We don't believe we are going to reverse the environmental crisis by simply passing laws. *We have to change the human understanding of its place and purpose in creation.* Unless you have that *fundamental change in values,* many of us believe environmental degradation will be irreversible." (67)

Consider this excerpt on redistribution of American wealth from NPRE's manifesto: *Earth's Climate Embraces Us All: A Plea From Religion and Science for Action on Global Climate Change*: "The wealthier nations of the planet have a solemn moral obligation to help developing countries protect the poor in their midst as they seek to limit greenhouse gas emissions." Gorman believes this "obligation" stems from Global

Warming's false predictions including "more frequent occurrences of heat waves, drought, torrential rains, and floods: (a) global sea level rise of between one-half and three feet; (an) increase of tropical diseases in now-temperate regions; (and) significant reduction in biodiversity." (68)

Just over thirty years ago some of these same scientists were predicting a coming Ice Age to unite the globe in submitting to world government and the loss of resources.

When they can't predict the weather for next week, it's awfully hard to predict what it will do a few decades from now.

The real purpose behind the infiltration of America's churches is to cultivate a neutering unity while gathering funds to support the cause of removing *only one God* from the public square: the Christian God upon whose laws America was founded and subsequently rose to become the most prosperous nation on earth. The churches are viewed as a windfall of funds for leftist causes of every immoral type from communism to pornography.

When George Washington was asked what makes America so prosperous, he answered, "Religion and morality are indispensible supports. In vain would that man claim the tribute of patriotism who would work to subvert these most basic pillars of society."

Paul Gorman, NRPE's Executive Director said the group now "represents the full and formal entry of the religious community into environmental work." Strangely, the partnership's office is located in the Cathedral of St. John the Divine, which is the same building that houses the Lindisfarne Association. (69)

In the *Training Manual for The Green Congregation Program, Revised edition,* October 2006, written by David Rhoads, sponsored by The Web of Creation, Lutheran School of Theology at Chicago provides "how to" instructions for clergymen and laymen to "green" their church congregations. In Part I: Getting Started and Keeping Going 11 steps are outlined that include developing an action plan in several areas: Worship; Education; Building and Grounds; Discipleship at Home and Work; and Public Ministry. Step nine says, "Consider a congregation project to benefit the community/city of location." Page 84 instructs comrades in political advocacy because global warming is a political tool for control.

Elizabeth Roberts and Elias Amidon, co-founders of the Earth Guild Interfaith-Fellowship, are the editors of *Earth Prayers From Around the World: 365 Prayers, Poems, and Invocations for Honoring the Earth*. A single sampling of the writings enclosed is this adapted could be demonstrated by Jane Pellowski in Anima Christi. Using elements of God's creation, she mocks Jesus Christ. The "earth prayers" are not a representation of responsible stewardship of the earth. They are an example of going over the edge into the pagan realm of earth-*worship*. (70)

Make no mistake: what we are witnessing in the world today is a struggle of the most epic proportions, Biblical proportions in fact, *to gain **dominion over the earth and everything in it.***

Global Earth Day, a pagan holiday created by the United Nations, is a *religious* day. The National Council of Churches Eco-Justice Working Group maintains a website with resources for pastors who work to transform their congregations into fools who worship the creation rather than the Creator. In 2004, this organization placed a "church bulletin insert" on their website titled "Life-giving Breath of God: Protecting the Sacred Gift of Air." A "Prayer of Confession" is offered where the "leader" says, "Giver of Life, in the midst of polluted air we groan with Creation… For the times we have failed to think of the harm done to air… For our reckless plundering and waste." To each of these phrases the congregation is instructed to respond, "Lord, have mercy." The "leader" continues later, "God, our Creator, you have made us one with this earth…" (71)

God has *not* made us *one* with the earth. We are each separate individuals who will die individually and be judged individually.

The most important difference between us and the earth:

We were created in the image of God...

We have the ability to think and choose.

Not choosing *is* choosing.

As recommended by G. Russell Evans, author of *Apathy, Apostasy and Apostles*, 1973:

TO GET YOUR CHURCH OUT OF THE NCC AND WCC:

Consider collecting signatures and then submitting the following:

RESOLUTION

WHEREAS, (Name of member denomination) is now a member of and a financial contributor to and supporter of the National Council of Churches of Christ in the United States of America, and the World Council of Churches; and

WHEREAS, the said National Council of Churches and the World Council of Churches have repeatedly and consistently engaged in secular and political activities (including lobbying) and have taken positions on secular and political subjects, giving the impression that in doing so they represent the millions of Christians who belong to their member churches; and

WHEREAS, the actions of the said church councils have exceeded the purposes for which they were organized, and are beyond the permissible area of conduct for non-profit charitable institutions; and

WHEREAS, the said councils (and groups and bodies under their sponsorship) have permitted certain policies and pronouncements to be formulated and promulgated which are not responsive to the member churches; and

WHEREAS, the positions and actions of these councils are not in accord with the thinking and wishes of (name of church, or group, or person); and

WHEREAS, past efforts to reform and control theses actions have been ineffective; and

WHEREAS, the ultimate effect of these activities of the said church councils has been embarrassment and anguish for individual members of (name and member denominations), and dissention within (name of member denomination), now therefore

BE IT RESOLVED THAT (name of church, or group, or person and address) concludes that continued membership of (name of member denomination) in the National Council of Churches and the World Council of Churches is no longer in the best interests of (name of member denomination) and that (name of member denomination) should therefore terminate all further financial support of both the said church councils and should withdraw its membership from them.

BE IT FURTHER RESOLVED THAT (name of church, or group, or person) shall submit this Resolution to (name of diocese or church conference or other appropriate governing body) with the request, recommendation and resolution to effectuate withdrawal of (name of member denomination) from the said National Council of Churches and the World Council of Churches.

Add lines for signatures, dates, the name of your church and its address.

References

NCC/WCC: Communist Fronts for Church Infiltration

1. Congressional Record--Appendix, pp. A34-A35
   January 10, 1963
   "Current Communist Goals," Extension of Remarks of
   Hon. A. S. Herlong, Jr. of Florida in the House of
   Representatives
2. PBS Publication: American Experience: "People and
   Events: Fundamentalism and the Social Gospel"
   pbs.org/wgbh/amex/monkeytrial/peopleevents/e_g
   ospel.html
3. Ibid
4. *Apathy, Apostasy and Apostles*, G. Russell Evans,
   1973, p. 19
5. Report: "Apostasy: The National Council of
   Churches," http://www.reformed-
   theology.org/html/issue07/apostasy.htm
6. Ibid, p. 19
7. Ibid, p. 20
8. Report: "Apostasy: The National Council of
   Churches," http://www.reformed-
   theology.org/html/issue07/apostasy.htm
9. *Apathy, Apostasy and Apostles,* G. Russell Evans,
   1973, p. 30
10. Ibid, pp. 20- 21
11. Report: "Apostasy: The National Council of
    Churches," http://www.reformed-
    theology.org/html/issue07/apostasy.htm
12. Ibid
13. Ibid
14. *Apathy, Apostasy and Apostles,* G. Russell Evans,
    1973, p. 22
15. Ibid, p. 23 & Office of Naval Intelligence Report
    dated September 15, 1935
16. Ibid, p. 23
17. Ibid, p. 23

18. "National Council of Churches: Worldviews, Activities, and Agendas," Jacob Laskin, 2005, http://www.discoverthenetworks.org/Articles/nccexpandedagenasactvi...

19. *"Introducing the World Council of Churches,"* Marlin VanElderen, 1992, p. 4

20. Report: "World Council of Churches (WCC)", http://www.discoverthenetworks.org/pintgroupProfile.asp?grpid+7514

21. *Apathy, Apostasy and Apostles,* G. Russell Evans, 1973, pp. 24-25

22. Ibid, p. 25

23. Ibid, p. 27

24. Report: "Apostasy: The National Council of Churches," http://www.reformed-theology.org/html/issue07/apostasy.htm

25. Ibid

26. Ibid

27. *Apathy, Apostasy and Apostles,* G. Russell Evans, 1973, p. 27

28. Ibid, p. 30

29. Ibid, pp. 34-35

30. Ibid, p. 38

31. Ibid, p. 82

32. Ibid, p. 81

33. Ibid, p. 82

34. Ibid, p. 44

35. Ibid, pp. 83-84

36. *Freedom's Lawmakers* , Eric Foner, 1996

37. *Apathy, Apostasy and Apostles,* G. Russell Evans, 1973, p. 84

38. National Council of Churches: Worldviews, Activities, and Agendas, Jacob Laskin, 2005, p.2, http://www.discoverthenetworks.org/Articles/nccexpandedagenasactvi...

39. Ibid

40. Ibid

41. Ibid

42. *By Stealth and Deception USA Transformation and its Parallel to the European Union*, Orlean Koehle, 2010, p. 481

43. "The Georgia Guidestones" RadioLiberty.com/stones.html

44. National Council of Churches: Group Profile, pp. 2-3, http://www.discoverthenetworks.org/groupProfile.asp?grpid=6916

45. Ibid

46. Ibid

47. Ibid

48. "National Council of Churches: Worldviews, Activities, and Agendas", Jacob Laksin, 2005: discoverthenetworks.org/groupProfile.asp?grpid+6916, p. 4

49. Ibid

50. Ibid

51. "The Church of Global Warming," http://archive.frontpagemag.com/read/Article.aspx?ARTID=29976

52. Ibid

53. "World Council of Churches Comes to U.S. Looking for 'Violence'" Mark Tooley, October 1, 2007, http://www.archive.frontpagemag.com/readArticle.aspx?ARTID=28306

54. Ibid

55. Ibid

56. Report: "National Council of Churches (NCC)" – Group Profile, http://www.discoverthenetworks.org/groupProfile.asp?grpid=6916

57. Ibid

58. Ibid

59. *By Stealth and Deception USA Transformation and its Parallel to the European Union*, Orlean Koehle, 2010, p. 481

60. Ibid, pp. 481-482

61. Ibid, p. 482
62. *Freedom on the Alter: The UN's Crusade Against God & Family*, William Norman Grigg, 1995, p. 170
63. "National Religious Partnership for the Environment (NRPE)" Group Profile, http://www.discoverthenetworks.org/groupProfile.asp?grpid=7572
64. Ibid
65. Ibid
66. Ibid
67. Ibid
68. "Paul Gorman" Individual Profile, http://www.discoverthenetworks.org/individualProfile.asp?indid=1673
69. *Freedom on the Alter: The UN's Crusade Against God & Family*, William Norman Grigg, 1995, p. 172
70. *Earth Prayers From Around the World: 365 Prayers, Poems, and Invocations for Honoring the Earth,* Elizabeth Roberts and Elias Amidon, 1991
71. webofcreation.org/ncc

www.ingramcontent.com/pod-product-compliance
Lightning Source LLC
Chambersburg PA
CBHW070618290526
45790CB00002B/938